W9-COB-725

This publication contains songs made famous by The Beatles.
The Beatles are not connected in any way with Northern Songs or its licensees.

Hal Leonard Publishing Corporation

7777 West Bluemound Road P.O. Box 13819 Milwaukee, WI 53213

ISBN 0-88188-598-3

THE BEATLES BEST

CONTENTS

ACROSS THE UNIVERSE

Words and Music by
JOHN LENNON and PAUL McCARTNEY

Slowly, and smoothly

Words are flow-ing out__ like end-less rain__ in-to a pa-per cup,__ they slith-er while__ they pass, they slip a-way____ a-cross the un-ni-verse.__

Pools of sor-row, waves of joy are drift-ing through my o-pened mind,__ pos -

CODA

D   F#m

Sounds of laugh - ter, shades of earth__ are ring - ing through my o-pened ears,__ in -

Em7   Gm   D

cit - ing and in - vit - ing me.__ Lim - it - less,__ un - dy - ing love, which

F#m   Em7

shines a - round__ me like a mil - lion suns, and calls me on and on__ a-cross__

A   A7   D

__ the u - ni - verse.__ Jai__ Gu - ru__ De -

ALL YOU NEED IS LOVE

Words and Music by
JOHN LENNON and PAUL McCARTNEY

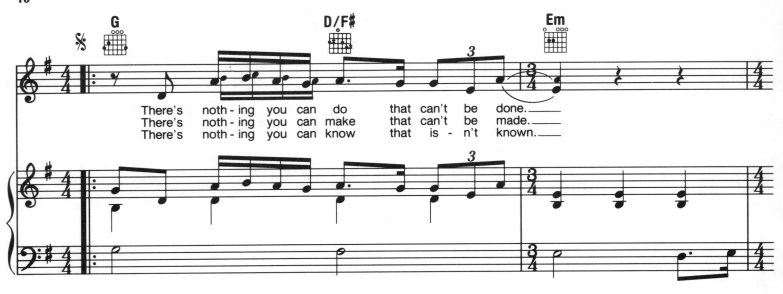

There's noth-ing you can do that can't be done.___
There's noth-ing you can make that can't be made.___
There's noth-ing you can know that is-n't known.___

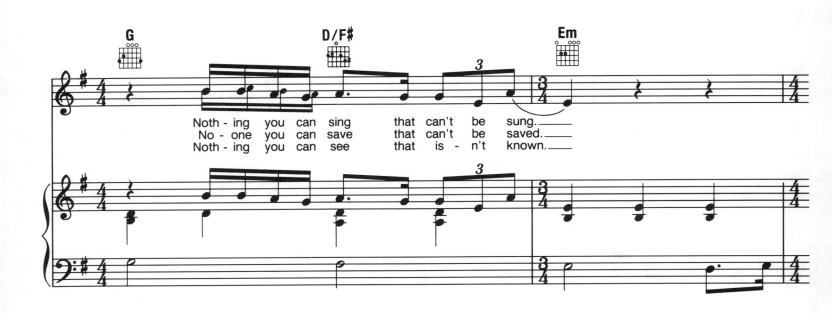

Noth-ing you can sing that can't be sung.___
No-one you can save that can't be saved.___
Noth-ing you can see that is-n't known.___

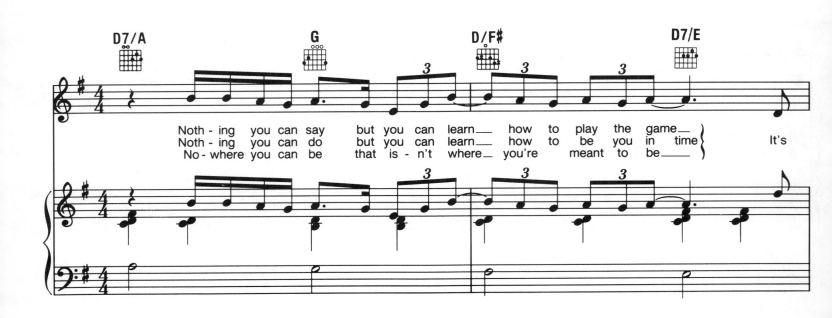

Noth-ing you can say but you can learn___ how to play the game
Noth-ing you can do but you can learn___ how to be you in time }
No-where you can be that is-n't where___ you're meant to be___

It's

D.S. al Coda

All My Loving

Words and Music by
JOHN LENNON and PAUL McCARTNEY

Brightly, with a swing feel

ALL TOGETHER NOW

Words and Music by
JOHN LENNON and PAUL McCARTNEY

One,   two,   three,   four,   can I have a-

AND I LOVE HER

Words and Music by JOHN LENNON
and PAUL McCARTNEY

BABY, YOU'RE A RICH MAN

Words and Music by
JOHN LENNON and PAUL McCARTNEY

How does it feel__ to be one of the beau - ti - ful peo - ple Now that you know__ who you are__ what do you want__ to be__ And have you trav - elled ve - ry far__ far as the eye__ can see__

ANYTIME AT ALL

Words and Music by
JOHN LENNON and PAUL McCARTNEY

BABY'S IN BLACK

Words and Music by
JOHN LENNON and PAUL McCARTNEY

though he'll nev-er come back, she's dressed in black.
though it's on-ly a whim, she thinks of him.

Oh, how long will it take till she sees the mis-take she has

made. Dear what can I do? Ba-by's in black and I'm_ feel-ing blue. Tell me

BACK IN THE U.S.S.R.

Words and Music by
JOHN LENNON and PAUL McCARTNEY

A
D

the way the pa-per bag was on my knee,___ Man___
it till to-mor-row to un-pack my case,___ Hon-
me hear your bal-a-lai-kas ring-ing out,___ Come___

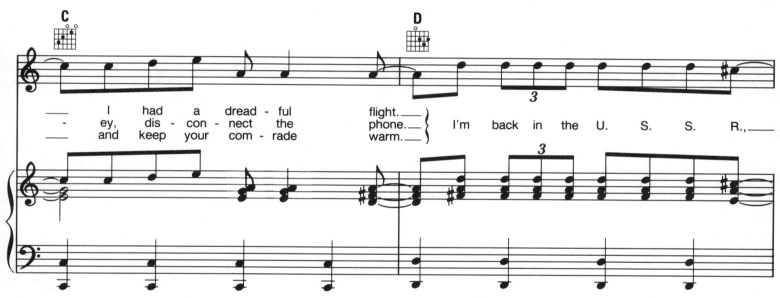

C
D

___ I had a dread-ful flight.___
-ey, dis-con-nect the phone. } I'm back in the U. S. S. R.,___
___ and keep your com-rade warm. }

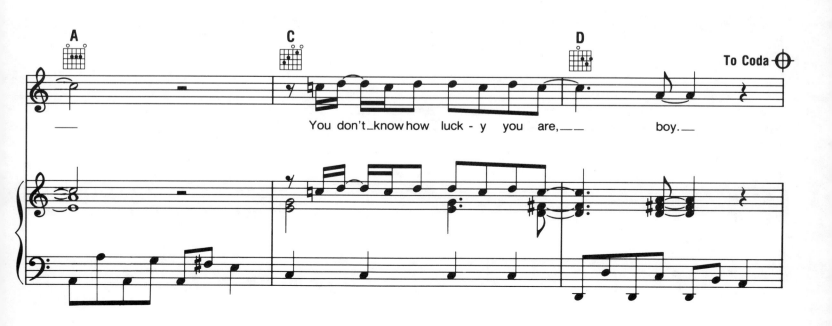

A
C
D

To Coda ⊕

You don't_know how luck-y you are,___ boy.___

THE BALLAD OF JOHN AND YOKO

Words and Music by
JOHN LENNON and PAUL McCARTNEY

1. Stand-ing in the dock at South-amp-ton, trying to get to Hol-land or France. The
2. Final-ly made the plane in-to Pa-ris, hon-ey-moon-ing down by the Seine. The
3. Pa-ris to the Am-ster-dam Hil-ton, talk-ing in our beds for a week. The

man in the mac said, "You've got to go back." You know they
Brown called to say, "You can make it O. K., You can get
news-peo-ple said, "Say, what're you do-ing in bed?" I said, "We're

Sav - ing up your mon - ey for a rain - y day,—

giv-ing all your clothes to char - i - ty. Last night the wife said,

"Oh boy, when you're dead you don't take noth-ing with you but your soul." _____ Think!

4. Made a light - ning trip to Vi - en - na,
5. Caught the ear - ly plane back to Lon - don,

BECAUSE

Words and Music by
JOHN LENNON and PAUL McCARTNEY

BIRTHDAY

Moderately Fast Rock

Words and Music by
JOHN LENNON and PAUL McCARTNEY

You say it's your birth - day,

It's my birth - day too,__ yeah;   They

say it's your birth - day.   We're gon - na have a good time;

I'm glad it's your birth - day,   Hap - py

birth - day to__ you.

BLACKBIRD

Words and Music by
JOHN LENNON and PAUL McCARTNEY

Black-bird sing-ing in the dead of night___
Black-bird sing-ing in the dead of night___

Take these bro-ken wings___ and learn to fly;___
Take these sunk-en eyes___ and learn to see;___

All your life___ you were on-ly wait-ing for this mo-ment to a -
All your life___ you were on-ly wait-ing for this mo-ment to be

CAN'T BUY ME LOVE

Words and Music by
JOHN LENNON and PAUL McCARTNEY

COME TOGETHER

Moderately slow, with a double-time feeling

Words and Music by
JOHN LENNON and PAUL McCARTNEY

Here come old flat-top, He come groov-ing up slow-ly, He got Joo Joo eye-ball, He one

ho-ly roll-er, He got hair down to his knee.___

Got to be a jok-er, He just do what he please.___

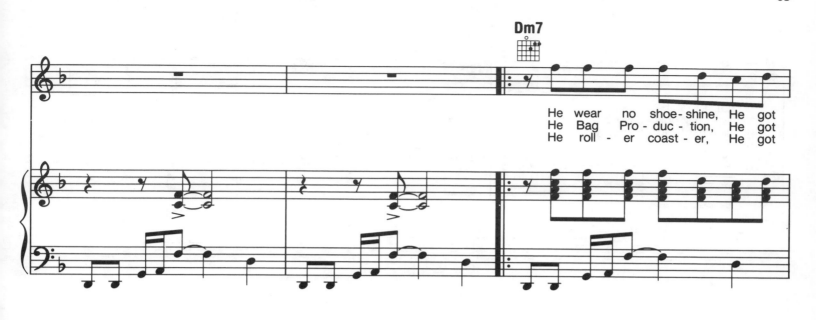

Dm7

He wear no shoe-shine, He got
He Bag Pro-duc-tion, He got
He roll-er coast-er, He got

toe - jam foot - ball, He got mon - key fin - ger, He shoot Co - ca Co - la, He say,
wal - rus gum-boot, He got O - no side-board, He one spi - nal crack-er, He got
ear - ly warn - ing, He got Mud - dy Wa - ter, He one Mo - jo fil - ter, He say,

A   **G7**   no chord

"I know__ you, you know me."__ One thing I can tell you is you
feet down be - low his knee.__ Hold you in his arm-chair, you can
"One and one and one is three." Got to be good look - ing 'cause he

DEAR PRUDENCE

Words and Music by
JOHN LENNON and PAUL McCARTNEY

beau - ti - ful___ and so are you.___ Dear_____ Pru - dence,___
you are part___ of ev - 'ry - thing.___ Dear_____ Pru - dence,___
let me see___ you smile a - gain.___ Dear_____ Pru - dence,___

won't you come out_____ to play?_____
won't you o - pen___ up your eyes?___
won't you let me see you smile?_____

Dear____
Dear____

Look a -

A DAY IN THE LIFE

Words and Music by
JOHN LENNON and PAUL McCARTNEY

76

DAY TRIPPER

Words and Music by
JOHN LENNON and PAUL McCARTNEY

Got a good rea-son
She's a big tea-ser,
Tried to please_ her,

for

A7

tak - ing the eas - y way out,___ Got a good rea - son
she took me half___ the way there.___ She's a big teas - er,
she on - ly played___ one-night stands.___ Tried to please___ her,

E7

for tak - ing the eas - y way out,___ now. She was a
she took me half___ the way there,___ now. She was a
she on - ly played___ one-night stands,___ now. She was a

F#

Day_____ Trip - per, one - way tick - et, yeah;___
Day_____ Trip - per, one - way tick - et, yeah;___
Day_____ Trip - per, Sun - day driv - er, yeah;___

DO YOU WANT TO KNOW A SECRET

Words and Music by
JOHN LENNON and PAUL McCARTNEY

Slowly and freely

You'll nev-er know how much I real-ly love you,

You'll nev-er know how much I real-ly care.

Moderately

List-en,

DON'T LET ME DOWN

Words and Music by
JOHN LENNON and PAUL McCARTNEY

Don't let me down,

Don't let me down.

Don't let me

down,

Don't let me down.

DRIVE MY CAR

Words and Music by
JOHN LENNON and PAUL McCARTNEY

Moderately, with a beat

Asked a girl what she
I told the girl what that my
I told that girl I could

want - ed to be.___
pros - pects were good,___
start right a - way,___

She said, "Ba - by, can't you see?___
And she said "Ba - by, it's un - der - stood.___
And she said, "Lis - ten babe, I got some - thing to say.___

I wan - na be fa - mous, a star of the screen,___
Work - ing for pea - nuts is all ver - y fine,___
I got no car and it's break - ing my heart,___

But you can do some - thing
But I can show you a
But I found a driv - er, and

ELEANOR RIGBY

Words and Music by
JOHN LENNON and PAUL McCARTNEY

EIGHT DAYS A WEEK

Words and Music by
JOHN LENNON and PAUL McCARTNEY

EVERY LITTLE THING

Words and Music by
JOHN LENNON and PAUL McCARTNEY

FIXING A HOLE

Words and Music by
JOHN LENNON and PAUL McCARTNEY

THE FOOL ON THE HILL

Words and Music by
JOHN LENNON and PAUL McCARTNEY

FOR NO ONE

Words and Music by
JOHN LENNON and PAUL McCARTNEY

FROM ME TO YOU

Words and Music by
JOHN LENNON and PAUL McCARTNEY

GET BACK

Words and Music by
JOHN LENNON and PAUL McCARTNEY

GETTING BETTER

Words and Music by
JOHN LENNON and PAUL McCARTNEY

GIRL

Words and Music by
JOHN LENNON and PAUL McCARTNEY

GOLDEN SLUMBERS

Words and Music by
JOHN LENNON and PAUL McCARTNEY

Once, there was a way to get back home-ward. Once, there was a way to get back home. Sleep pret-ty dar-ling, do not

CARRY THAT WEIGHT

Words and Music by
JOHN LENNON and PAUL McCARTNEY

Boy, _____ you're gon - na car - ry that weight, _____ car - ry that weight _____ a long _____

time. Boy, _____ you're gon - na car - ry that weight, _____

car - ry that weight, _____ a long _____ time.

Good Day Sunshine

Words and Music by
JOHN LENNON and PAUL McCARTNEY

GOT TO GET YOU INTO MY LIFE

Words and Music by
JOHN LENNON and PAUL McCARTNEY

Very steady, with a swing feel

I was a- lone, I took a ride, I did- n't know what I would find there.
You did- n't run, you did- n't lie, you knew I want- ed just to hold you.
What can I do, what can I be, when I'm with you I want to stay there.

An- oth- er road, where may- be I
And had you gone you knew in time
If I'm true I'll nev- er leave

Got to get you in-to my life!___

Repeat and Fade

HAPPINESS IS A WARM GUN

Words and Music by
JOHN LENNON and PAUL McCARTNEY

A HARD DAY'S NIGHT

Words and Music by
JOHN LENNON and PAUL McCARTNEY

HELTER SKELTER

Words and Music by
JOHN LENNON and PAUL McCARTNEY

Moderate Rock

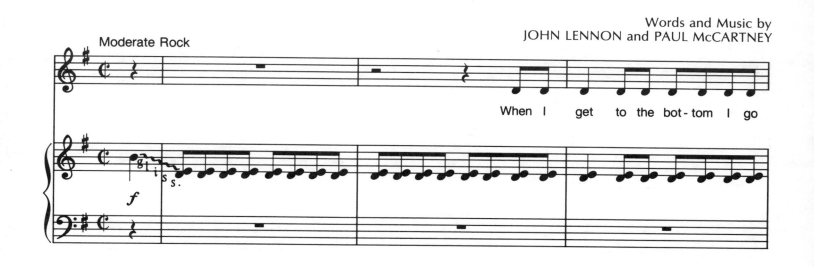

When I get to the bot-tom I go

back to the top of the slide,— Where I stop and I turn, and I go for a ride,—

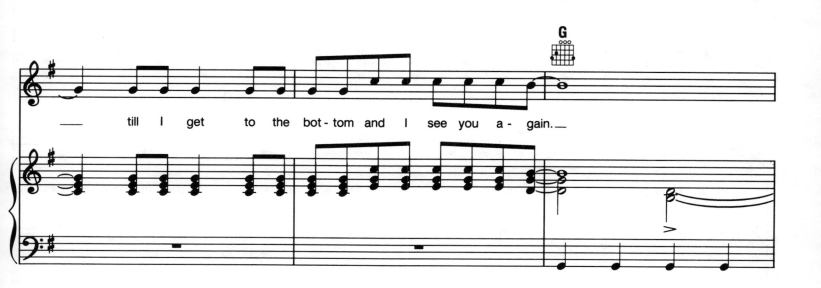

— till I get to the bot-tom and I see you a-gain.—

Look out! 'cause here she come!

A E

A Em

When I

E7 A/E

get to the bot-tom, I go back to the top of the slide,_ And I stop and I

HELLO, GOODBYE

Words and Music by
JOHN LENNON and PAUL McCARTNEY

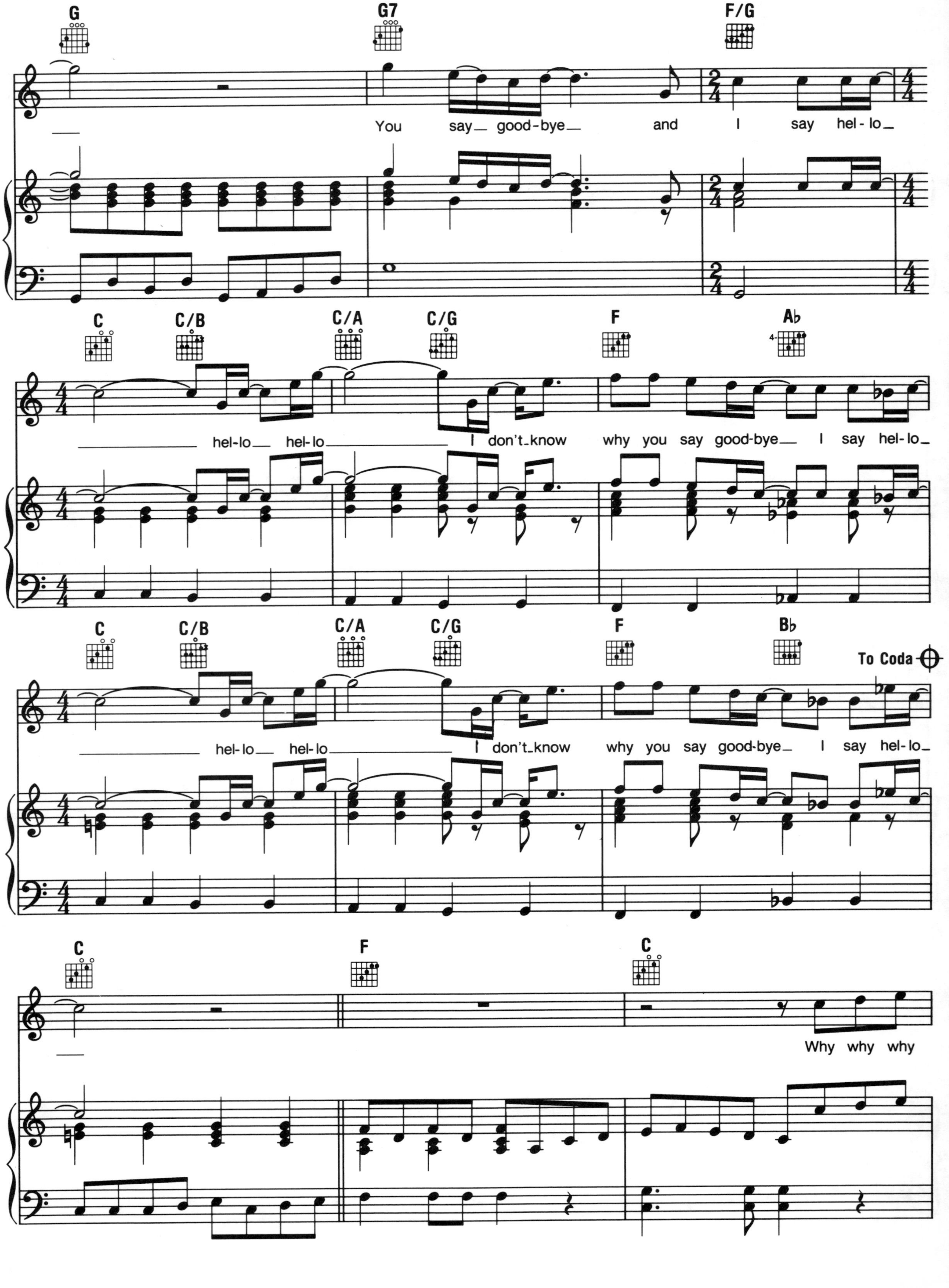

G
G7
F/G
You say good-bye and I say hel-lo
C
C/B
C/A
C/G
F
A♭
hel-lo hel-lo I don't know why you say good-bye I say hel-lo
C
C/B
C/A
C/G
F
B♭
To Coda
hel-lo hel-lo I don't know why you say good-bye I say hel-lo
C
F
C
Why why why

HELP!

Words and Music by
JOHN LENNON and PAUL McCARTNEY

Moderately, with a driving beat

Help! I need some-bod - y, Help! Not just an - y - bod - y, Help! You know I need some - one, ___ Help! ___

no chord

HERE COMES THE SUN

Words and Music by
GEORGE HARRISON

Here comes— the sun,—

Here comes— the sun,—— and I say "It's all—— right."

Sun, sun, sun, here it comes.

HONEY PIE

Words and Music by
JOHN LENNON and PAUL McCARTNEY

She was a work-ing girl North of Eng-land way. (Half spoken) Now she's hit the big time In the U. S. A. And if she could on-

HERE, THERE AND EVERYWHERE

Words and Music by JOHN LENNON
and PAUL McCARTNEY

HEY JUDE

Words and Music by JOHN LENNON
and PAUL McCARTNEY

I AM THE WALRUS

Words and Music by
JOHN LENNON and PAUL McCARTNEY

I DON'T WANT TO SPOIL THE PARTY

Words and Music by
JOHN LENNON and PAUL McCARTNEY

love her. If I find her I'll be glad,—

I still love her. {Oh, I don't

want to spoil the par - ty, so I'll go.—— I would
had a drink or two and I don't care.—— There's no

hate my dis - ap - point - ment to show.—— There's
fun in what I do if she's not there.—— I

I FEEL FINE

Words and Music by
JOHN LENNON and PAUL McCARTNEY

I WANNA BE YOUR MAN

Words and Music by
JOHN LENNON and PAUL McCARTNEY

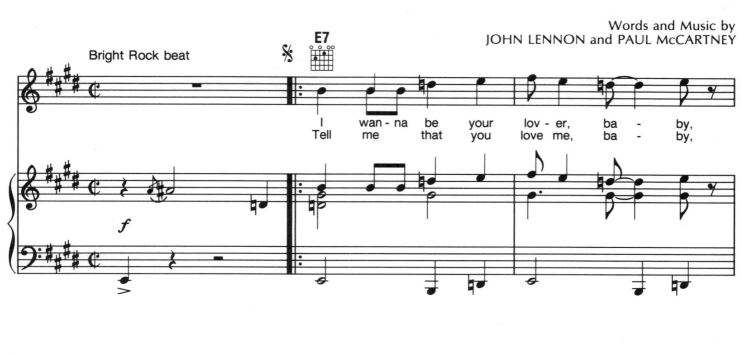

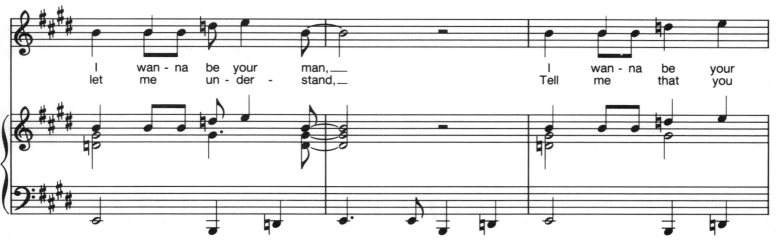

I wan-na be your man,—

I SAW HER STANDING THERE

Bright Rock

Words and Music by
JOHN LENNON and PAUL McCARTNEY

I SHOULD HAVE KNOWN BETTER

Words and Music by
JOHN LENNON and PAUL McCARTNEY

I WANT TO HOLD YOUR HAND

Words and Music by
JOHN LENNON and PAUL McCARTNEY

MCA MUSIC PUBLISHING

I WANT YOU
(SHE'S SO HEAVY)

Words and Music by
JOHN LENNON and PAUL McCARTNEY

I WILL

Words and Music by
JOHN LENNON and PAUL McCARTNEY

I'LL FOLLOW THE SUN

Words and Music by
JOHN LENNON and PAUL McCARTNEY

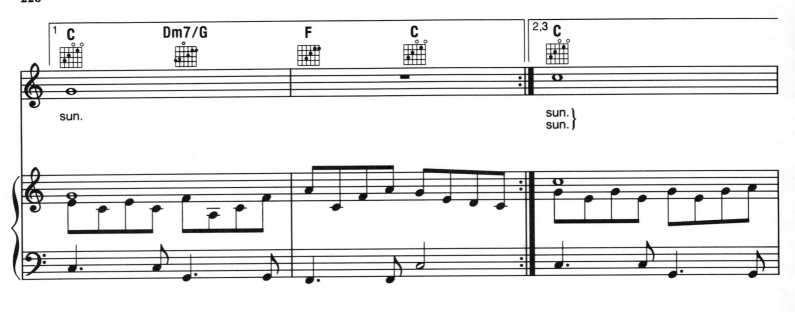

sun.   sun.
                                                  sun.

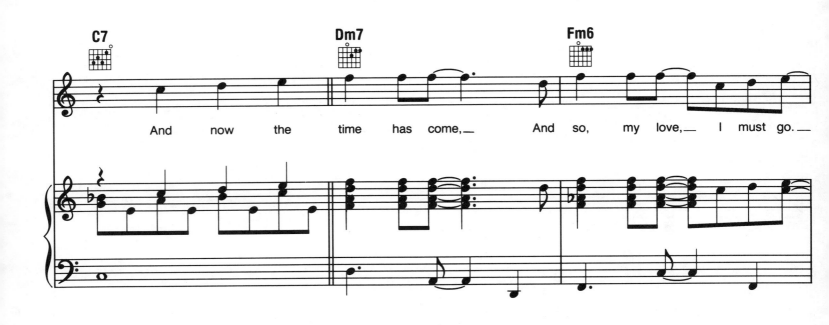

And now the time has come,___ And so, my love,___ I must go.___

___   And though I lose a friend___

I'LL BE BACK

Words and Music by
JOHN LENNON and PAUL McCARTNEY

I'LL CRY INSTEAD

Words and Music by
JOHN LENNON and PAUL McCARTNEY

I'M A LOSER

Words and Music by
JOHN LENNON and PAUL McCARTNEY

I'M LOOKING THROUGH YOU

Words and Music by
JOHN LENNON and PAUL McCARTNEY

I'm look-ing through you,

Your lips are mov-

you, where did you go?

-ing, I can-not hear.

I'M HAPPY JUST TO DANCE WITH YOU

Words and Music by
JOHN LENNON and PAUL McCARTNEY

I'VE JUST SEEN A FACE

Words and Music by
JOHN LENNON and PAUL McCARTNEY

I've just seen a face I can't for-get the time___ or place where we just

IF I FELL

Words and Music by
JOHN LENNON and PAUL McCARTNEY

If I fell in love with you would you prom - ise to be true And

help me un - der - stand__ 'Cause I've been in love be - fore And I

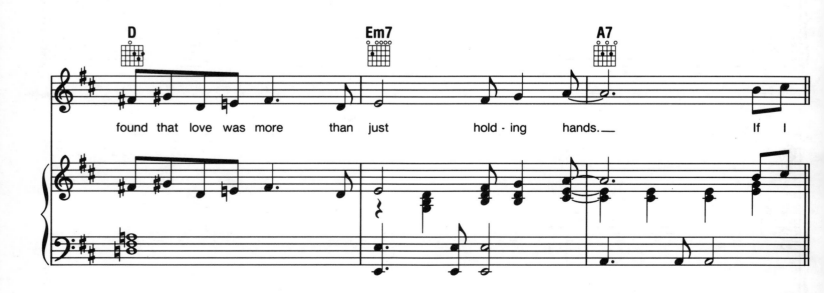

found that love was more than just hold - ing hands.__ If I

IN MY LIFE

Words and Music by
JOHN LENNON and PAUL McCARTNEY

There are plac - es I'll re - mem - ber all my
But of all these friends and lov - ers there is

life,_____ though some have changed.__ Some for - ev - er, not for
no_____ one com - pares with you.__ And these mem - 'ries lose for their

bet - ter; Some have gone_____ and some re - main.__ All these
mean - ing when I think of_ love as some - thing new.__ Tho' I

IT WON'T BE LONG

Words and Music by
PAUL McCARTNEY

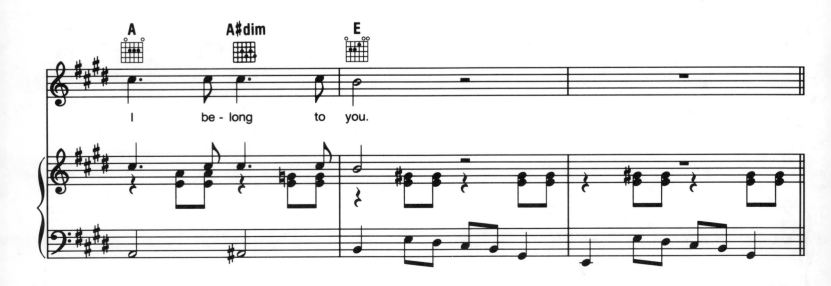

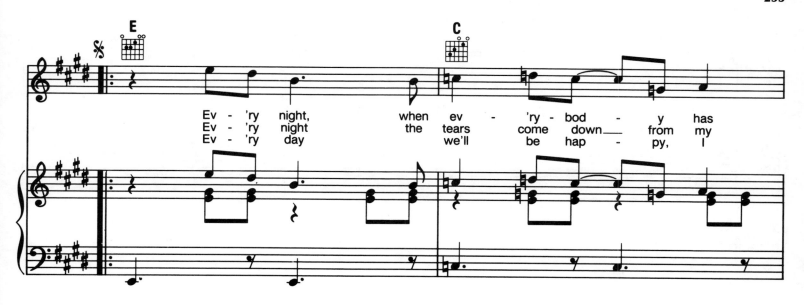

Ev - 'ry night,   when ev - 'ry - bod - y has
Ev - 'ry night   the tears come down__ from my
Ev - 'ry day   we'll be hap - py, I

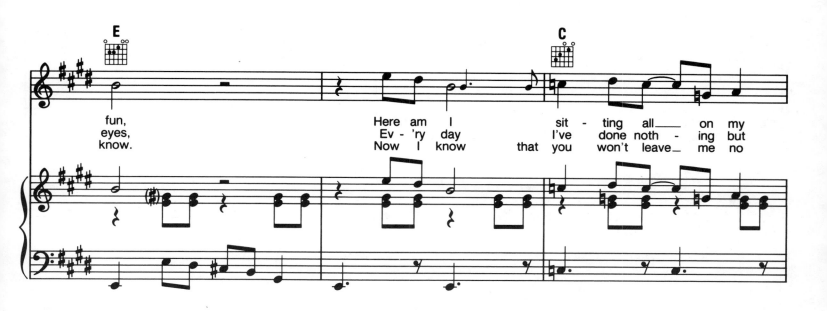

fun,
eyes,   Here am I   sit - ting all__ on my
know.   Ev - 'ry day   I've done noth - ing but
          Now I know   that you won't leave__ me no

own.
cry.
more.   It won't be

IT'S ONLY LOVE

Words and Music by
JOHN LENNON and PAUL McCARTNEY

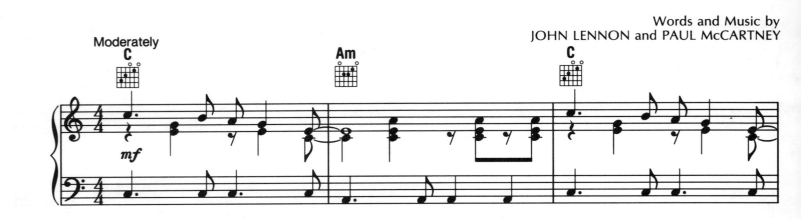

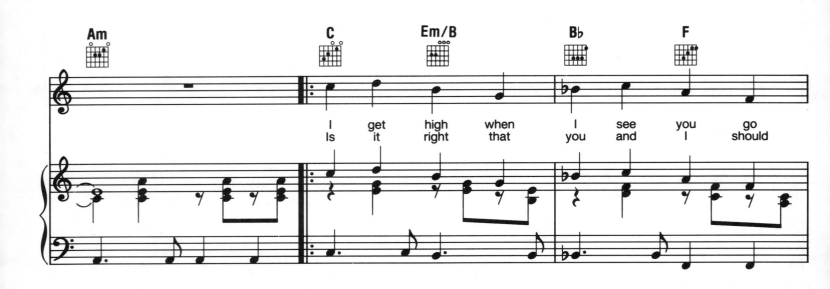

Is I get it high right when that I you see and you I go should

by, My oh my. When you sigh, my,
fight ev-'ry night? Just the sight of

LET IT BE

Words and Music by
JOHN LENNON and PAUL McCARTNEY

When I find my-self in times of trou-ble

Instrumental

Moth-er Mar-y comes to me Speak-ing words of wis-dom, Let it

be ____ and in my hour of dark-ness She is

JULIA

Words and Music by
JOHN LENNON and PAUL McCARTNEY

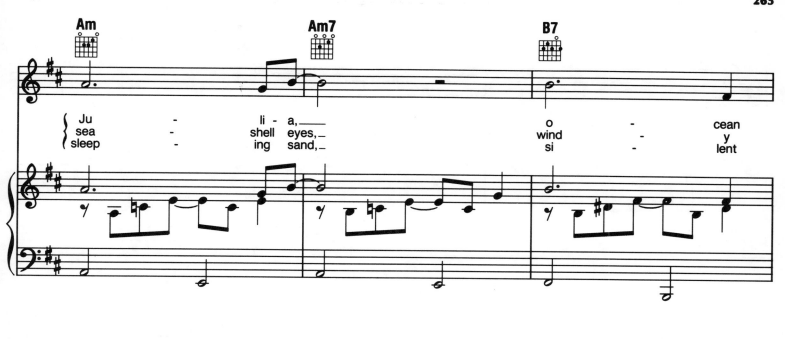

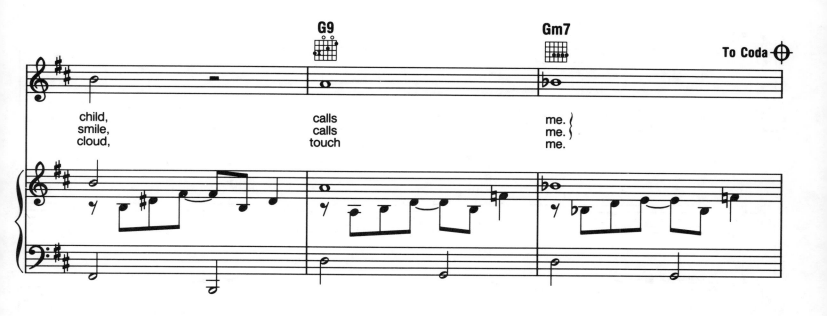

LADY MADONNA

Words and Music by
JOHN LENNON and PAUL McCARTNEY

Friday night ___ ar - rives ___ with - out ___ a
3. Tues - day af - ter - noon ___ is nev - er

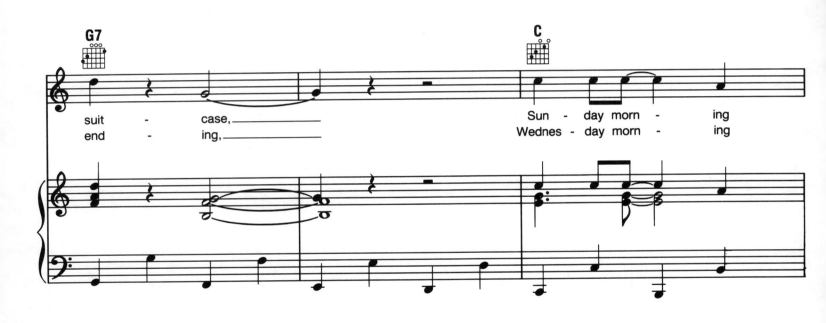

suit - case, ___
end - ing, ___

Sun - day morn - ing
Wednes - day morn - ing

creep - ing like a nun, ___
pa - pers did - n't come, ___

Mon - day's child has
Thurs - day night your

THE LONG AND WINDING ROAD

Words and Music by JOHN LENNON
and PAUL McCARTNEY

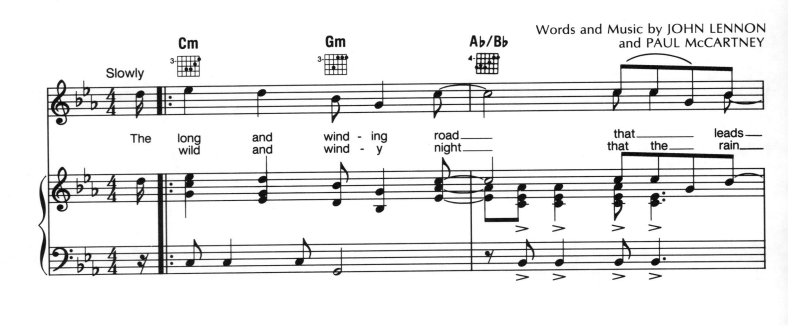

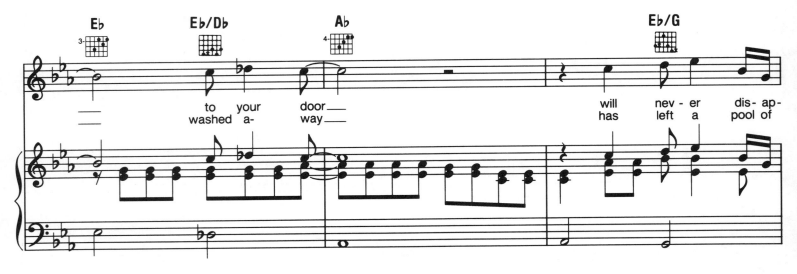

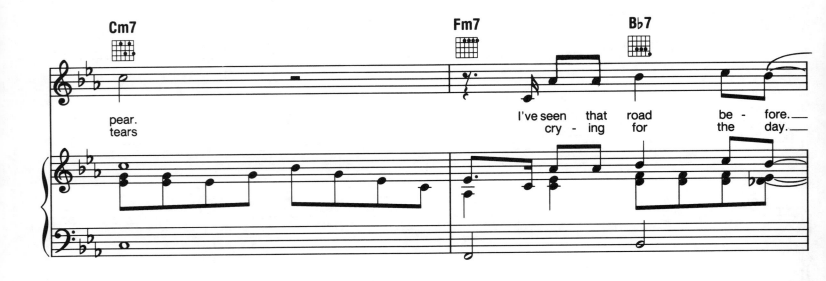

LOVE ME DO

Words and Music by
JOHN LENNON and PAUL McCARTNEY

Love, love me do, ___ you know I love you, ___ I'll al - ways be true, ___ so please ____

LOVELY RITA

Words and Music by
JOHN LENNON and PAUL McCARTNEY

me - ter   maid.

LUCY IN THE SKY WITH DIAMONDS

Words and Music by
JOHN LENNON and PAUL McCARTNEY

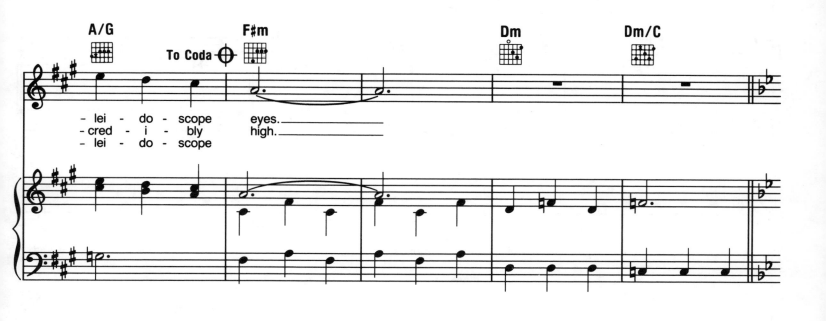

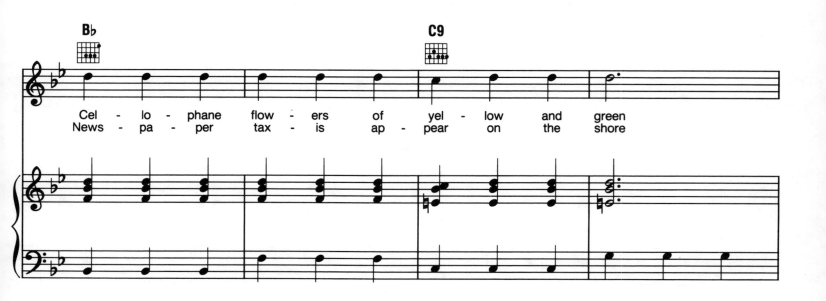

289

MAGICAL MYSTERY TOUR

Words and Music by
JOHN LENNON and PAUL McCARTNEY

Roll up, roll up for the Magical Mystery Tour.
Step right this way.

Roll up, _____

Roll up ___ for the mys-

-ter-y tour. ___

Roll up, _____

MARTHA MY DEAR

Words and Music by
JOHN LENNON and PAUL McCARTNEY

Mar - tha,___ my dear,___

Mar - tha,___ my dear,___ you have al - ways been my in - spi -

MAXWELL'S SILVER HAMMER

Moderately (played as)

Words and Music by
JOHN LENNON and PAUL McCARTNEY

Joan was quiz-zi-cal, stud-ied pat-a-phys-i-cal
Back in school a-gain, Max-well plays the fool a-gain,
P. C. Thir-ty-one said, "We've caught a dir-ty one,"

sci-ence in the home___ Late nights all a-lone___
teach-er gets an-noyed.___ Wish-ing to a-void___
Max-well stands a-lone.___ Paint-ing tes-ti-mo-

___ with a test-tube, oh, oh, oh, oh.
___ an un-pleas-ant sce-e-e-ene,___
-ni-al pic-tures, oh, oh, oh, oh.___

Max - well   Ed - i - son,   ma - jor - ing in med - i - cine,
She   tells   Max to stay   when the class has gone a - way.
Rose   and   Val - er - ie   scream - ng from the gal - ler - y

calls   her on the phone:__   "Can   I   take   you out__
So he waits   be - hind__   Writ - ing   fif - ty   times__
say   he must   go   free.__   The judge   does   not   a - gree__

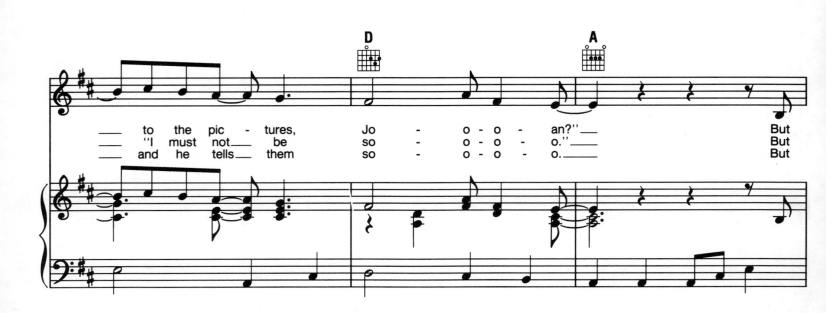

__ to the pic - tures,   Jo - o - o - an?"   But
__ "I must not__ be   so - o - o - o."__   But
__ and he tells__ them   so - o - o - o.   But

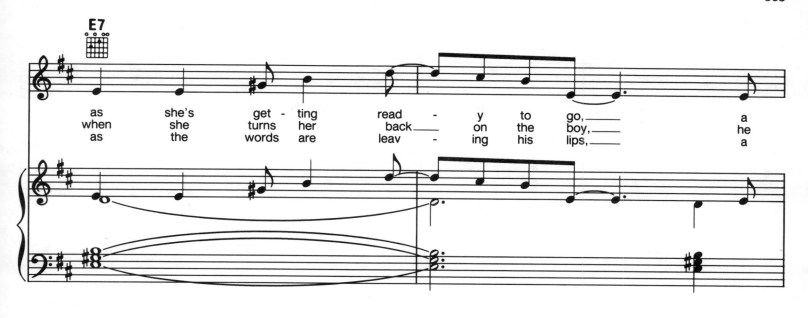

E7

as she's get - ting read - y to go, _____ a
when she turns her back _____ on the boy, _____ he
as the words are leav - ing his lips, _____ a

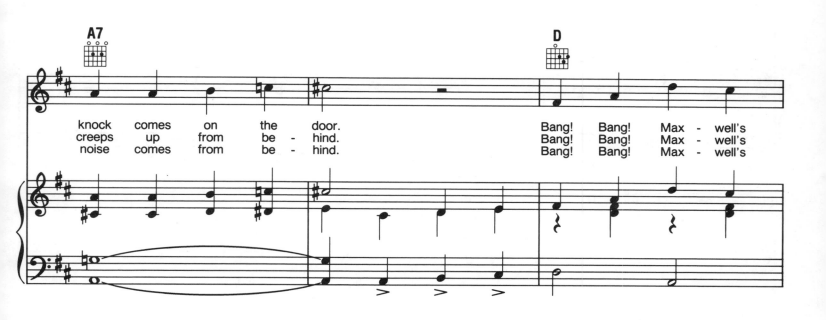

A7　　　　　　　　　　　　　　　　　　　　**D**

knock comes on the door. Bang! Bang! Max - well's
creeps up from be - hind. Bang! Bang! Max - well's
noise comes from be - hind. Bang! Bang! Max - well's

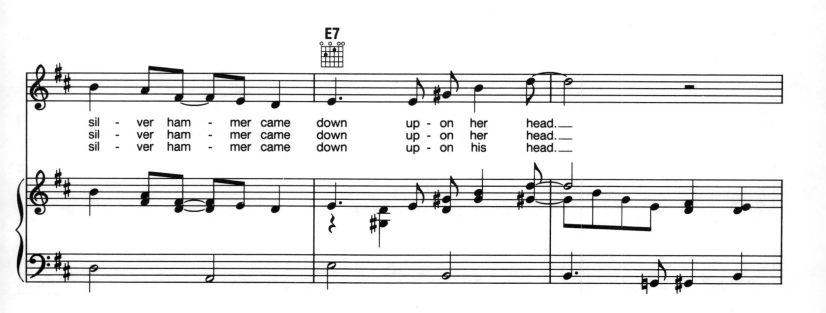

E7

sil - ver ham - mer came down up - on her head. _____
sil - ver ham - mer came down up - on her head. _____
sil - ver ham - mer came down up - on his head. _____

Sil - ver ham - mer.

MEAN MR. MUSTARD

Words and Music by
JOHN LENNON and PAUL McCARTNEY

POLYTHENE PAM

Words and Music by
JOHN LENNON and PAUL McCARTNEY

Well, you should see Pol-y-thene Pam, she's so good-look-ing but she looks like a man.__ Well, you should see her in drag,__ dressed in her pol-y-thene bag,__ Yes, you should see Pol-y-thene Pam.

Yeah,   yeah,   yeah.

SHE CAME IN THROUGH THE BATHROOM WINDOW

Words and Music by
JOHN LENNON and PAUL McCARTNEY

She came in through the bath-room win-dow,
And so I quit the p'lice de-part-ment,

pro-tect-ed by a sil-ver spoon.
and got my-self a stead-y job.

But now she sucks her thumb and won-ders by the
And though she tried her best to help me. she could

NO REPLY

Words and Music by
JOHN LENNON and PAUL McCARTNEY

MICHELLE

Words and Music by
JOHN LENNON and PAUL McCARTNEY

NORWEGIAN WOOD
(THIS BIRD HAS FLOWN)

Words and Music by
JOHN LENNON and PAUL McCARTNEY

Moderately

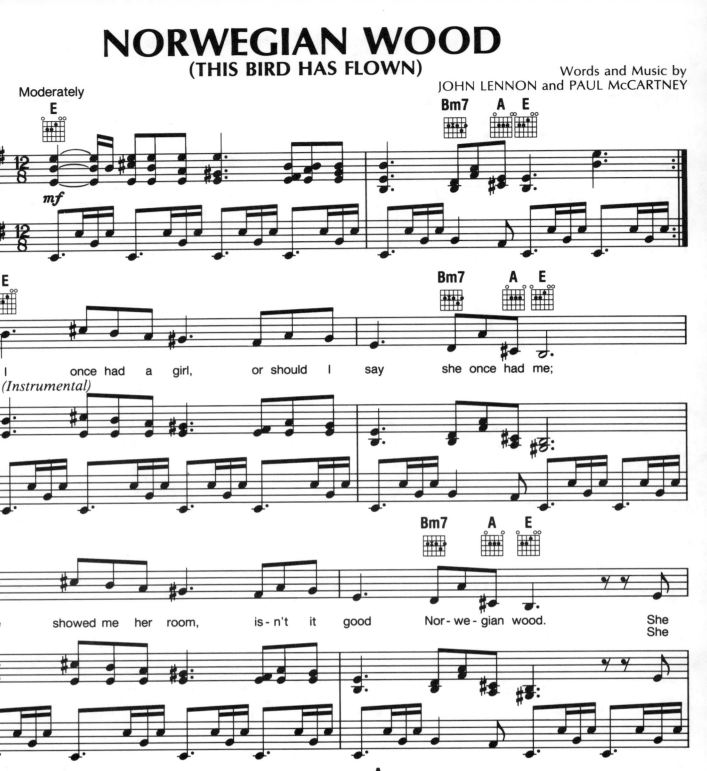

I once had a girl, or should I say she once had me;

(Instrumental)

She showed me her room, is-n't it good Nor-we-gian wood. She
She

asked me to stay and she told me to sit an-y-where,
told me she worked in the morn-ing and start-ed to laugh,

So
I

NOWHERE MAN

Words and Music by
JOHN LENNON and PAUL McCARTNEY

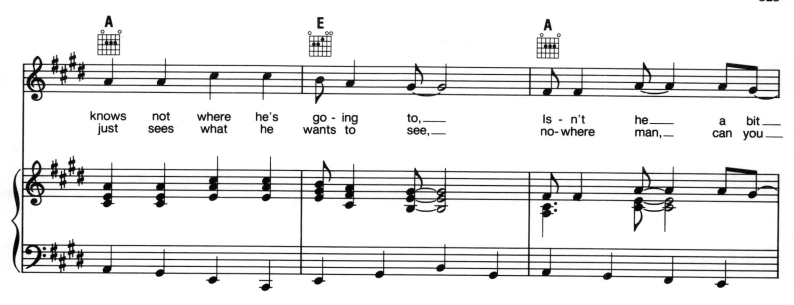

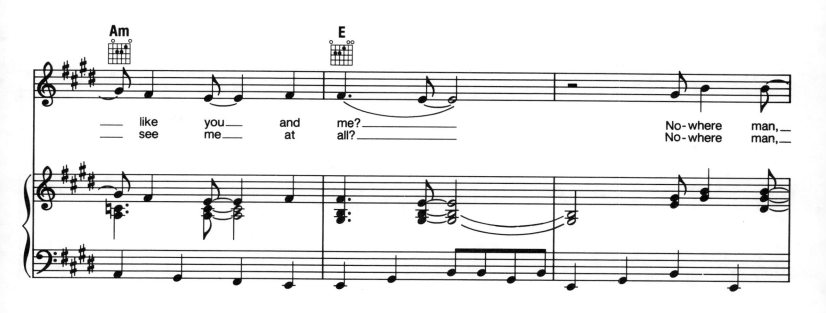

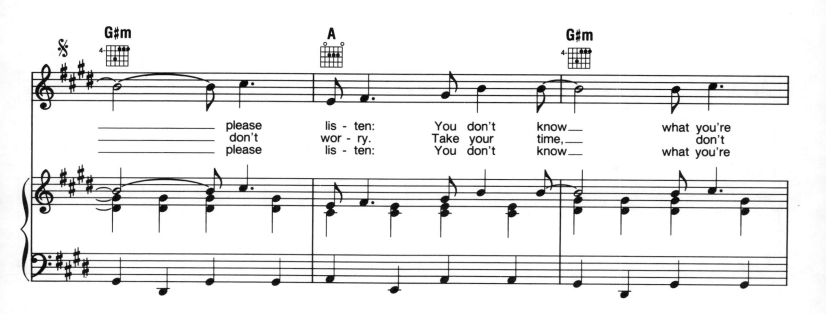

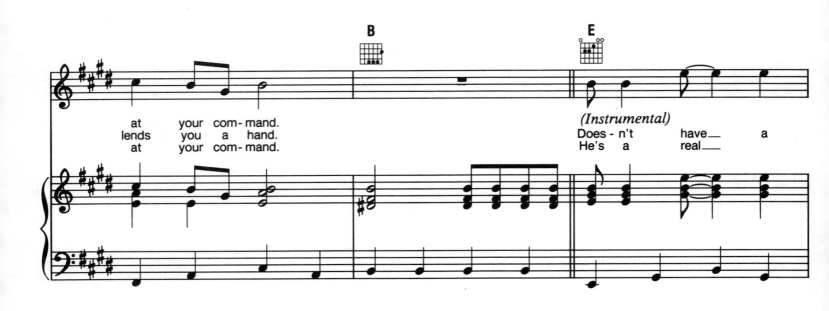

OB-LA-DI, OB-LA-DA

Words and Music by
JOHN LENNON and PAUL McCARTNEY

OCTOPUS'S GARDEN

Words and Music by
RICHARD STARKEY

PENNY LANE

Words and Music by JOHN LENNON
and PAUL McCARTNEY

corner is a bank-er with a mo-tor-car;__ The lit-tle chil-dren laugh at him be-hind his
Lane: the bar-ber shaves an-oth-er cus-tom-er,__ We see the bank-er sit-ting wait-ing for a

back. And the bank-er nev-er wears a mac__ in the pour
trim. And then the fire-'man rush-es in__ from the pour-

-ing rain, ve-ry strange! Pen-ny Lane__ is in my ears
-ing rain, ve-ry strange! Pen-ny Lane__ is in my ears

__ and in my eyes,__ wet be-neath the blue__
__ and in my eyes,__ there be-neath the blue__

OH! DARLING

Words and Music by
JOHN LENNON and PAUL McCARTNEY

P.S. I LOVE YOU

Words and Music by
JOHN LENNON and PAUL McCARTNEY

As I write this let-ter, send my love to you. Re-mem-ber that I'll

PAPERBACK WRITER

Words and Music by
JOHN LENNON and PAUL McCARTNEY

Bright Rock

Pa - per - back wri - ter, pa - per - back wri - ter.

Dear_ Sir or Mad - am will you read my book? It took me
It's a thou - sand pag - es, give or take a few; I'll be

dirt - y man, ___ and his cling - ing wife ___ does-n't un - der-stand. His
have the rights, ___ it could make a mil - lion for you o - ver-night. If you

son is work - ing for the Dai - ly Mail; ___ It's a
must re - turn ___ it you can send it here, ___ But I

C

stead - y job ___ but he wants to be a pa - per-back writ - er, ___
need a break ___ and I want to be a pa - per-back writ - er, ___

G7

__ pa - per-back writ - er.
__ pa - per-back writ - er.

PLEASE PLEASE ME

Moderately with a beat

Words and Music by
JOHN LENNON and PAUL McCARTNEY

1.3. Last night I said these words to my girl,

2. You don't need me to show the way love,

I know {you/I} nev-er e-ven

Why do I al-ways have to

try,_____ girl.

say,_____ love.

Come on (Come on)____ Come,

RAIN

Words and Music by
JOHN LENNON and PAUL McCARTNEY

REVOLUTION

Words and Music by
JOHN LENNON and PAUL McCARTNEY

You   say   you   want   a   rev - o - lu -
say   you   got   a   real   so - lu -
say   you'll   change   the   con - sti - tu -

- tion,_____   Well_____   you   know,_____   We   all   want
- tion,_____   Well_____   you   know,_____   We'd   all   love _____
- tion,_____   Well_____   you   know,_____   We   all   want

ROCKY RACCOON

Moderately, in two (♩ = 1 beat)

Words and Music by
JOHN LENNON and PAUL McCARTNEY

(Spoken:) Now somewhere in the Black Mountain Hills of Dakota
eye. Rocky didn't like that. He said: "I'm going

there lived a young boy named Rocky Raccoon. So one And one day his
to get that boy." day one he walked into

woman ran off with another guy, hit young Rocky in the
town and booked himself a room in the local saloon.

help with good Rock-y's re-vi-val.

SEXY SADIE

Words and Music by
JOHN LENNON and PAUL McCARTNEY

RUN FOR YOUR LIFE

Words and Music by
JOHN LENNON and PAUL McCARTNEY

SGT. PEPPER'S LONELY HEARTS CLUB BAND

Moderately slow, but with a strong beat

Words and Music by
JOHN LENNON and PAUL McCARTNEY

SHE LOVES YOU

Words and Music by
JOHN LENNON and PAUL McCARTNEY

SHE'S A WOMAN

Words and Music by
JOHN LENNON and PAUL McCARTNEY

SHE'S LEAVING HOME

Words and Music by
JOHN LENNON and PAUL McCARTNEY

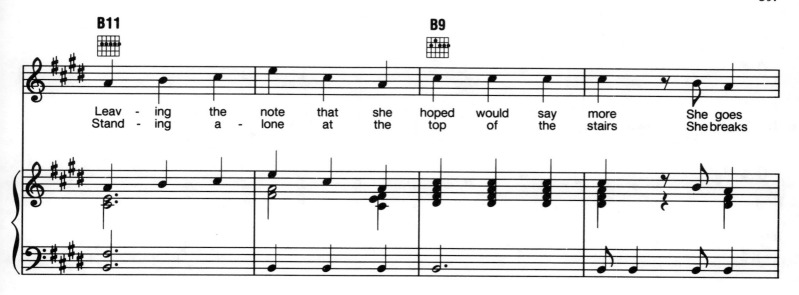

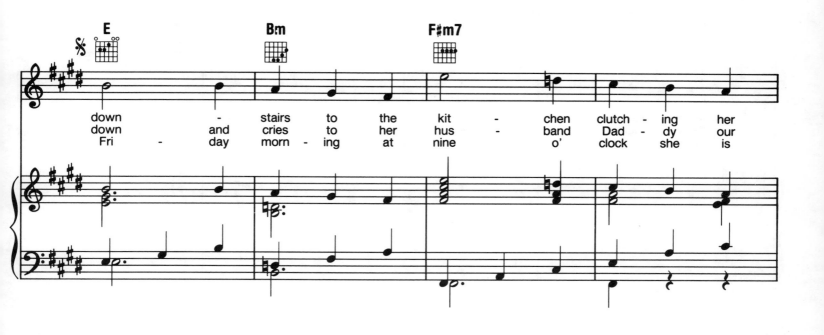

Qui - et - ly turn - ing the back - door key___
Why would she treat us so thought - less - ly___
Wait - ing to keep the ap - point - ment she made

Step - ping out - side she is free
How could she do this to me
Meet - ing a man from the mo - tor trade

She___ (We gave her most of our___ lives) is
She___ (We nev - er thought of our___ selves) is
She___ (What did we do that was___ wrong) is

SOMETHING

Words and Music by
GEORGE HARRISON

Some-thing in the way she moves,
Some-where in her smile she knows,
Some-thing in the way she knows,

at-tracts me like no oth-er lov-er.
that I don't need no oth-er lov-er.
and all I have to do is think of her.

Some-thing in the way she woos me.
Some-thing in her style that shows me.
Some-thing in the things she shows me.

I don't want to leave her now, you

STRAWBERRY FIELDS FOREVER

Words and Music by
JOHN LENNON and PAUL McCARTNEY

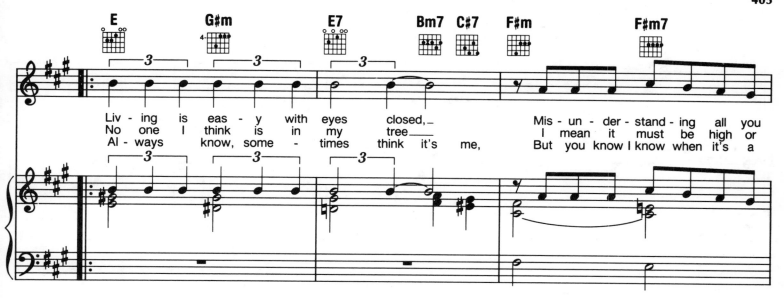

Liv - ing is eas - y with eyes closed,
No one I think is in my tree
Al - ways know, some - times think it's me,

Mis - un - der - stand - ing all you
I mean it must be high or
But you know I know when it's a

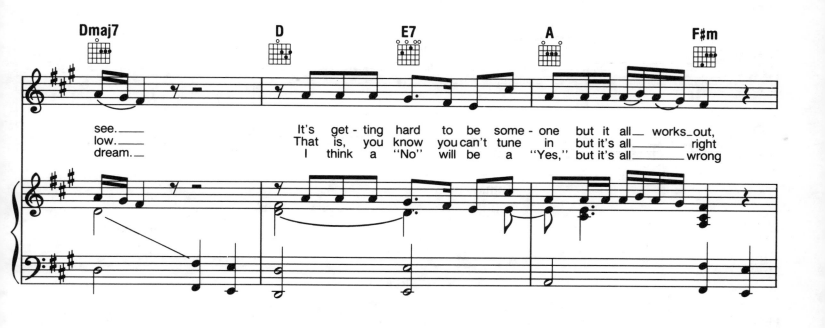

see.
low.
dream.

It's get - ting hard to be some - one but it all works out,
That is, you know you can't tune in but it's all right
I think a "No" will be a "Yes," but it's all wrong

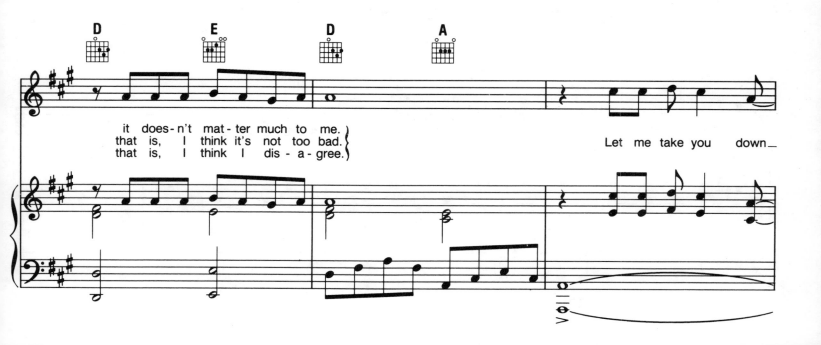

it does - n't mat - ter much to me.
that is, I think it's not too bad.
that is, I think I dis - a - gree.

Let me take you down

TAXMAN

Words and Music by
GEORGE HARRISON

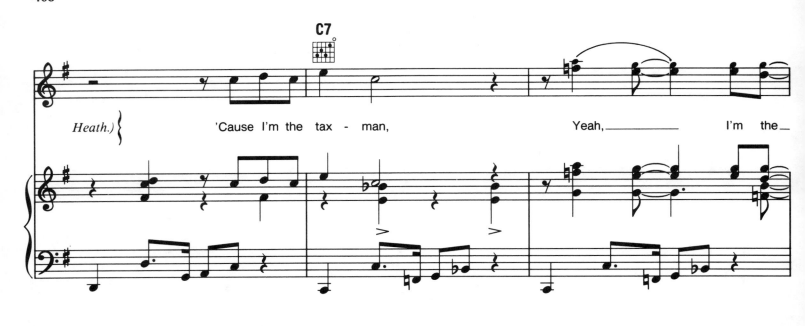

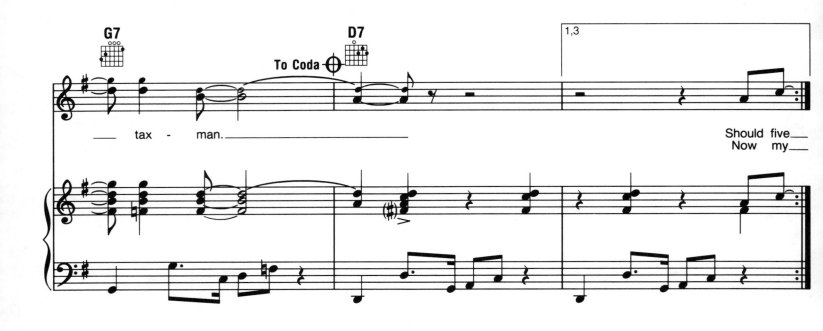

SUN KING

Words and Music by
JOHN LENNON and PAUL McCARTNEY

TELL ME WHY

Words and Music by
JOHN LENNON and PAUL McCARTNEY

Tell me why _____ you cried. ____

and why you lied _____ to me. ____

Tell ____ me why _____ you cried, ____

THANK YOU GIRL

Words and Music by
JOHN LENNON and PAUL McCARTNEY

THERE'S A PLACE

Words and Music by
JOHN LENNON and PAUL McCARTNEY

Moderately bright

There _____ is a place where I can go when I feel low, when I feel blue. And it's my mind,

THINGS WE SAID TODAY

Words and Music by
JOHN LENNON and PAUL McCARTNEY

You say you will love me, if I have to go, You'll be thinking of me some-how I will know.

You say you'll be mine, 'til the end of time, These days such a kind girl, seems so hard to find.

THIS BOY
(RINGO'S THEME)

Words and Music by
JOHN LENNON and PAUL McCARTNEY

Moderate Ballad

mf

D · **Bm** · **Em** · **A7**

Dmaj7 · **Bm** · **Em** · **A7**

That boy _____ took my love _____ a -
That boy _____ is - n't good _____ for

Dmaj7 · **Bm** · **Em** · **A7**

way.
you, Oh, he'll re - gret it _____ some
Tho' he may want _____ you

Dmaj7 · **Bm** · **Em7** · **A7**

day, _____ But this boy _____ wants you back a -
too, _____ This boy _____ wants you _____ back a -

TICKET TO RIDE

Words and Music by
JOHN LENNON and PAUL McCARTNEY

I think I'm gon - na be sad,_____ I think it's to - day___
said that liv - ing with me_____ is bring - in' her down___

_____ yeah!___ The girl that's driv - ing me mad___
_____ yeah!___ For she would nev - er be free___

___ is go - ing a - way.___ } She's got a tick - et to ride,__
___ when I was a - round.

TWIST AND SHOUT

Words and Music by
BURT RUSSELL and PHIL MEDLEY

TWO OF US

Words and Music by
JOHN LENNON and PAUL McCARTNEY

1. Two of us, rid - ing no - where, spend - ing some - one's hard - earned pay.
2. Two of us, send - ing post - cards, writ - ing let - ters, on my wall.
3,4. Two of us, wear - ing rain - coats, stand - ing so - lo, in the sun.

WE CAN WORK IT OUT

Words and Music by
JOHN LENNON and PAUL McCARTNEY

Try to see it my way, do I have to keep on talk - ing
Think of what you're say - ing, you can get it wrong and still you

till I can't go on? While you see it your way, run a risk of know - ing that our
think that it's all right. Think of what I'm say - ing, we can work it out and get it

love may soon be gone.
straight, or say good - night. We can work it out, we can work it out.

WHILE MY GUITAR GENTLY WEEPS

Words and Music by
George Harrison

WHEN I'M SIXTY FOUR

Words and Music by
JOHN LENNON and PAUL McCARTNEY

WITH A LITTLE HELP FROM MY FRIENDS

Words and Music by JOHN LENNON
and PAUL McCARTNEY

THE WORD

Words and Music by
JOHN LENNON and PAUL McCARTNEY

WHY DON'T WE DO IT IN THE ROAD

Words and Music by
JOHN LENNON and PAUL McCARTNEY

Why don't we do it in the road?

Why don't we do it in the road?

Why don't we do it in the road?

Why don't we do it in the road?

YES IT IS

Words and Music by
JOHN LENNON and PAUL McCARTNEY

1. If you wear red to-
2. Scar-let were the clothes she

night, re-mem-ber what I said to
wore, ev-'ry-bod-y knows I'm

night, For red is the col-or that my
sure, I would re-mem-ber all the

YELLOW SUBMARINE

Words and Music by
JOHN LENNON and PAUL McCARTNEY

YESTERDAY

Words and Music by JOHN LENNON
and PAUL McCARTNEY

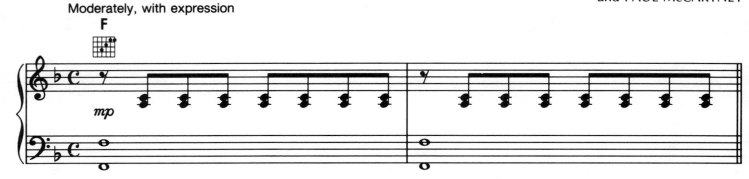

Moderately, with expression

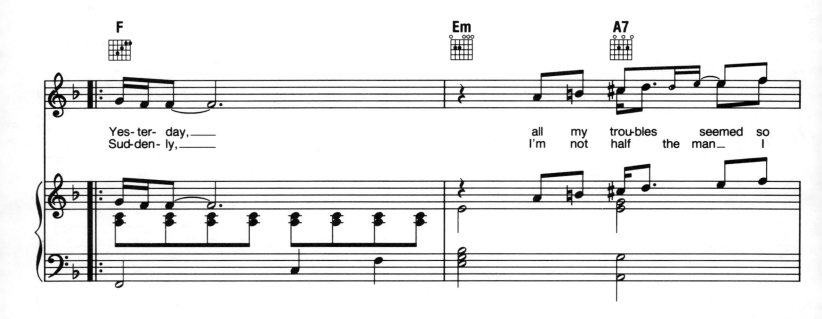

Yes-ter- day,____ all my trou-bles seemed so
Sud-den- ly,____ I'm not half the man__ I

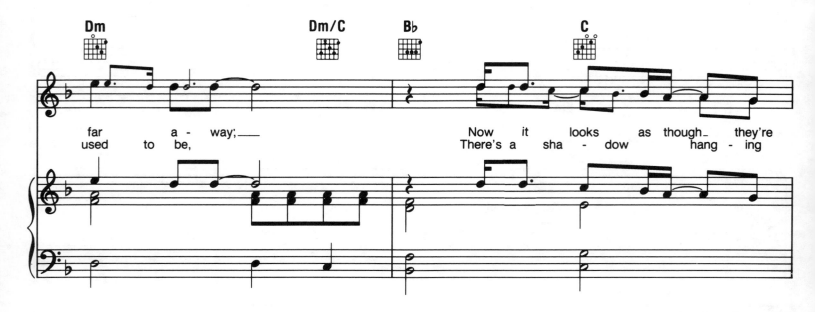

far a - way;____ Now it looks as though__ they're
used to be, There's a sha-dow hang - ing

YOU CAN'T DO THAT

Words and Music by
JOHN LENNON and PAUL McCARTNEY

YOU NEVER GIVE ME YOUR MONEY

Words and Music by
JOHN LENNON and PAUL McCARTNEY

You nev-er give me your mon - ey,
I nev-er give you my num - ber,

You on-ly give me your fun - ny pa - per,
I on-ly give you my sit-u-a - tion,

And in the mid-dle of ne-
And in the mid-dle of in-

YOU WON'T SEE ME

Words and Music by
JOHN LENNON and PAUL McCARTNEY

When I call ___ you up, ___ why you ___

your line's ___ en-gaged. ___ I have had ___
should want ___ to hide. ___ But I can't ___

e-nough. ___ so act ___ your age. ___
get through. ___ my hands ___ are tied. ___

YOU'RE GOING TO LOSE THAT GIRL

Words and Music by
JOHN LENNON and PAUL McCARTNEY

You're gon-na lose that girl.___ You're gon-na lose that girl.___

If you don't take her out to-night,___ she's gon-na
If you don't treat her right my friend,___ you're gon-na

YOU'VE GOT TO HIDE YOUR LOVE AWAY

Words and Music by
JOHN LENNON and PAUL McCARTNEY

Moderately (in 2)

YOUR MOTHER SHOULD KNOW

Words and Music by
JOHN LENNON and PAUL McCARTNEY